The World's Greatest Backyard Games

MATTHEW GREAR

prensa·press

The Definitve Guide to the World's Top Yard Games

by Matthew Grear

The World´s Greatest Backyard Games

Copyright © 2021 by Matthew Grear

Published by Prensa Press
Mexico City, Mexico · Chicago, IL
www.prensa.press

Cover design and illustrations copyright © by Polly Jiménez
Book design by Polly Jiménez
Edited by Paul Biasco

For more information contact: info@prensa.press

First hardcover edition June 2021
Printed in China

ISBN 978-1-7332402-2-2 (hardcover)

Distributed by SCB Distributors

This book is dedicated to my mom and dad, who taught me that life is too short. Get out there and have some fun!

Introduction

Growing up with a dad who was only 5'2'', I knew at a very young age that professional sports were not going to be in the cards for me.

I remember it like it was yesterday. It was a warm summer evening, and my father had just taken me to Pee Wee football signups. During the weigh-in, the coaches told us I didn't weigh enough to play with the kids my age and instructed my dad to sign me up with the boys in the younger age group. On our way home, I was devastated. After pouting for 15 minutes, I asked my dad why I couldn't play on the same team as my friends. All he said was, "Matt, did you see how much taller the coaches are than me? You're part Italian, you'll be lucky if you make it taller than 5'6''. He wasn't wrong. I topped out at a whopping 5'6" and ¾ inches.

That didn't keep me from competing. As a kid and into my college years, I tried almost every sport known to man. I challenged myself by participating in rec league, intramural, and school sports. What kept me coming back was the camaraderie and the desire to compete. I'm pretty sure the added benefit of running around provided an additional sense of peace for my ADHD self.

The biggest draw was the sense of being on a team. There is nothing better than strategizing with teammates on how to defeat the opposition. The faith you put in them to pick you up while you are down and trust that they will do what is expected makes sports special. What I lacked in size, I needed to make up for with strategy, and that became my game plan.

As I got older, tailgating became the norm on weekends. While in college at the University of Missouri, I played cornhole religiously on Saturdays. My slice of heaven was equipped with a black and gold board that featured Truman the Tiger's head painted right in the middle. The bags had a flawless slide and were perfectly plump. They left that beautiful chalky cloud when they slammed on the board. It was as if a mini firework was going off each time they landed.

During my Sophomore year, I switched gears and transferred to the University of Illinois. Besides occasionally going to class to take a deep dive into a lecture on the Krebb's Cycle, I learned a whole new set of games. Polish Frisbee and KanJam took center stage. It was not uncommon for my friends and I to have a day-long tournament in our front yard. Let's just say this turned into a good source of income for me, but I never lost sight of the classics.

Since the Midwest is a kind of melting pot, everyone I met seemed to have their own favorite. They all had a slightly different set of rules or a different nickname for the games that I had grown to love.

It wasn't until October 2014, on my first ever Euro trip, that I found my calling for yard games. While strolling through a park in Amsterdam, I noticed a group of people playing something I'd never seen before. This game involved throwing wooden batons at other wooden blocks. I soon learned they were playing Kubb. Being the annoying American that I am, I went right up to the group and asked if I could play. They gave me a few throws and just like that, I was hooked. Immediately after I left, I began to wonder what other games were out there that I didn't know about yet?

What other games could I dominate my friends in? My journey to discover the best backyard games from around the world began on that very day!

Backyard games have steadily become an essential aspect of today's society. From getting people off their couches and into the fresh air for some exercise or to simply socialize with friends, yard games provide limitless benefits. They even provide a perfect escape mechanism at family parties when the dreaded "What's new in your life?" question from your aunt pops up. Most importantly, games bring people together.

For millennia, games have played a role in human development, binding us as teams and as fans. Some of the oldest games even involved the use of human bones as playing pieces. Historians argue that games are the oldest form of social interaction. They have been used to settle disputes, enrich religious ceremonies, develop strategic thinking, and even as preparation for battle. Today a concept of "gamification" has swept the corporate world. Companies offer badges and trophies for their users to move up the ranks and compete in virtual challenges. In whatever context or country you find yourself in, there are games to be played.

The purpose of this book is to spread the joy of yard game culture from around the world and to inspire people to get outside and try something new. So the next time the weather is nice, pick out a game from this book and go have some fun. I hope you enjoy reading this book as much as I enjoyed writing it. Please feel free to share your yard game stories, pictures, and games on Instagram with @Yardgamesworld or on our website www.yardgamesworld.com.

Badminton
England

HISTORY

Badminton's roots run deep, stretching into some of the oldest and far-reaching places on Earth including Greece, China, and India.

All of those primitive versions of the game that influenced modern Badminton shared one common trait that remains today — the shuttlecock.

The shuttlecock, also known as a bird or birdie, was traditionally made with feathers attached to a sole or weighted ball or disk. The first version of *jianzi*, a shuttlecock-based game in China, was played in the 5th century B.C.

Although versions of the shuttlecock-based sport can be traced to those countries listed above, the official country of origin under the name of Badminton in the Encyclopedia Britannica is linked to the country estate of the dukes of Beaufort.

The fine folks in Gloucestershire, England, a bit more than 100 miles West of London, are thought to have played the first official game of badminton in 1873.

The game has come a long way from the early days of pomp and circumstance and is more likely to be found smack dab in the middle of a Labor Day grill-out or, more infamously, in a two-week stretch of high school gym class.

Jianzi

Badminton became an official Olympic sport in 1992.

SETUP

Each player should be supplied with a stringed racket that resembles a tennis racket but slightly smaller.

A shuttlecock consisting of half a round ball at one end and feathers or feather-like material on the other end.

A net should be set at a height of 5'1".

The full width of the court is 20 ft. For a singles game, the width is 17 ft. The length of the court is 44 ft.

HOW TO PLAY

2 or 4 players

• Badminton can be played as a singles or doubles match.

• The server must hit the shuttlecock over the service line and into the box opposite the side they are serving from.

• Players must swing the racket underhand while serving.

• If the serving side loses a rally, the server passes the shuttlecock to their opponent.

SCORING

Games are played to 21 points.
The winning team must win by 2.

Bocce
Italy

HISTORY

Bocce, one of the world's oldest yard games, dates back to a discovery made more than 7,000 years ago in Egypt. Sir Francis Petrial, an English scientist, discovered a painting of two boys playing a game that resembled Bocce in a tomb. Scientists later dated that painting to 5200 B.C.

According to the World Bocce League, the game's path spread throughout Palestine and into Asia Minor, later became popular with the Greeks and finally the Romans. The game's current rules date back to B.C. 246 during the Roman Punic Wars.

It was the Greeks who brought Bocce to Italy, where it exploded in popularity. Today it can be found being played in cities and villages across the country and, more recently, around the world.

Some of the most famous figures of history are known to have enjoyed the art of Bocce, including Galileo Galilei, Leonardo Da Vinci, the Greek physician Hippocrates, Sir Francis Drake, and Queen Elizabeth.

While the early Roman version of the game involved coconuts from Africa, today's game involves wood.

The term Bocce is derived from the Italian word *boccia*, which translates to bowl. If the history of Bocce tells us anything, it's that lawn bowling is here to stay.

SETUP

A set of eight large Bocce balls is needed, as well as a smaller object ball called a *pallino*.

Any playing surface can be used as long as it is level. Traditionally Bocce is played on natural soil, but grass, gravel, and packed dirt will suffice.

HOW TO PLAY

2 to 8 players

- Players form two teams of up to four players.
- One player chosen at random starts the game by throwing the pallino from one end of the court to the other.
- A player from that team begins the game and attempts to throw a ball as close to the pallino as possible.
- The other team then tosses, and the teams continue rotating throws until all the balls have been thrown.

SCORING

Games are played to 7 or 13 points.

Only one team scores per frame. 1 point is awarded for each ball that is closer to the pallino than the nearest ball thrown by the opposing team.

Brilli
Malta

HISTORY

Sundays on the tiny Maltese island of Gozo are for Brilli.

The bowling-like game that is played on the streets of the nation's smaller island off the coast of southern Italy dates back to the 15th century before the arrival of the Knights of St. John.

People on Gozo argue that Brilli is an older game than the famed Italian sport of Bocce.

Brilli has a special place in the hearts and culture of Gozitans, and streets are blocked off on Sundays to make way for the players and their observers.

While the game isn't widely known around the world, Maltese players are attempting to get the game listed on the National Cultural Heritage List.

Brilli is similar to many worldly games that involve the use of pins known as skittles. What makes this game unique is the inclusion of a central pin called an *Is-Sultan* that is worth nine points and the values of the corner pins and middle row pins being different.

Another unique twist in Brilli is that if a player's point total goes above 24 points, they are immediately out.

SETUP

Players should set up nine Brilli, or wooden pins, in a square formation with three rows of three.

The Is-Sultan pin in the middle has a small sphere at the top to distinguish itself.

One wooden ball is needed for play.

The four Brilli at the corners are called *Is-Secondi*, and the four remaining Brilli, excluding the central Is-Sultan, are called *Qarmuc*.

The central Brilli is worth 9 points. The corner Brilli are worth 6 points, and the remaining Brilli are worth 1 point each.

HOW TO PLAY

2 to 8 players

• Players choose a starting place for the first throw, and the first player takes their turn throwing the ball toward the Brilli. Pins knocked down during the first throw are worth double. The first player then gets a second throw from where the ball landed following the first throw.

• Each succeeding player takes his or her own turn during the first round following these rules.

• If no player reaches 24 on their first round, a second round begins, and the scoring changes.

• The first player to reach exactly 24 points wins.

SCORING

During the first throw of the first round, all scoring counts as double. If a player knocks down two Brilli of different values on a turn, each pin is only worth 2 points.

During the second round, point values for the Brilli change, and only the Is-Sultan is worth 2 points. The rest of the Brilli are worth 1.

Caliche
Spain

HISTORY

Caliche is a traditional game of accuracy that was born in Murcia in the southeast of Spain.

The game, often referred to as Caliche Murciano, gained its title from the name of the wooden cylinder that is placed at the center of the field of play which must be knocked over with pieces of metal or coins.

The earliest documentation of the game dates back more than 300 years in the region, and the game has continued to be played in the traditional style ever since.

The goal of Caliche is to knock down both the central cylinder and the *moneda*, a large metal disc or coin, on top of the wooden cylinder.

Games can be played individually, but it is more common for pairs of two to compete.

Locals of Spanish villages where the game is still played are trying to prevent the game from going extinct by introducing it to residents at a young age.

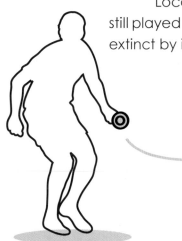

SETUP

A Caliche, or cylindrical piece of wood, should be placed standing up at the end of the field of play approximately 35 feet from the throwing line.

A metal disc or coin should be placed atop the Caliche.

Eight round metal discs are needed to throw.

HOW TO PLAY

4 players

• The aim of the game is first to hit the Caliche so as to let the moneda drop and second, to throw the remaining monedas as near as possible to the moneda that fell from the top of the cylinder.

• Each team of two takes four throws per turn.

• Once a player knocks the moneda from the Caliche, that player throws their additional coins, attempting to land them as close to the moneda as possible.

• For each coin that lands closer to the moneda than the caliche, that team is awarded one point.

• The first team to four points wins.

Chaskele
Ghana

Ghana

Africa

HISTORY

Chaskele is an indigenous game played primarily in Ghana, but the relatively simple rules and equipment needed to play mean the game has worldwide appeal.

Chaskele is in many ways similar to cricket, with a bit of baseball and golf mixed in. It involves using cans in the place of balls, a bucket, and a stick or bat.

It is, in reality, the backyard version of the international sport of cricket and has been a favorite of children in Ghana for decades.

While one player seeks to toss a smashed can into a container, typically a bucket or tire, the "defender" of that container is equipped with a stick and attempts to swat the can as far as they can away from the goal.

The game is typically played with at least five players and the last one to land their can in the bucket is the loser.

SETUP

Players should set up a container or goal in an open area using either a bucket, tire, or other object with a large opening.

Each player should then crush a can to use as their throwing device.

HOW TO PLAY

2 to 15 players

- In the first round of play, all players line up at a baseline 5 steps away from the goal, and each player takes a free throw trying to land their crushed can or metal plate into the goal.
- The player or players who made their free throw then stand in front of or around the goal and defend it with a bat or stick.
- Those who did not make the initial free throw will attempt to score again. This time with the defenders batting away their attempts.
- Players must throw their can or plate from where it lands if defended.
- This continues until everyone's can or plate has made it into the goal.
- The last one to score is the loser.

SCORING

There is no scoring. The last player to make their can or plate into the goal is the loser.

Cherokee Marbles
North America/Cherokee Nation

HISTORY

The game of Cherokee Marbles has been passed down through countless generations of Cherokee members in the American southeast region. It has remarkably been able to retain its traditional roots and rules into the modern age.

The game, which is pronounced *Di-ga-da-yo-s-di* in the Cherokee language, dates back to around 800 A.D. and has remained one of the most popular Native American games in existence.

Cherokee Marbles were originally crafted from stone. Pieces were chipped away to form spheres about the size of billiard balls.

Most current players of the game have substituted the stone balls, which are extremely time-consuming to form, for actual billiard or snooker balls out of convenience.

The complex game of accuracy is played on a five-hole course and is traditionally played by adults.

The goal is to finish the course's sequence of holes first, either as an individual or as a team, and then return to the starting point.

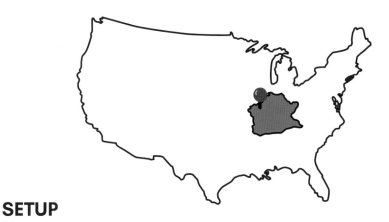

SETUP

Players should set up a five-hole course making the holes 10 to 40 feet apart, forming an L-shape. The field should be approximately 100 feet long. Holes should be 2 inches in diameter and dug shallowly into the ground.

Each player should have their own marble.

HOW TO PLAY

2 - unlimited players

• Teams are decided by throwing a marble from the second hole back to the first. Players whose marbles are closest to the first hole are placed on the same team. Team games are traditionally played with two or three players to a team.

• Once the teams are picked, players from each team take turns throwing their marble underhand toward each sequential hole. A player must rest their marble exactly atop the hole to advance to the next hole. Once a player has made it in the second hole, they can backtrack and play defense, hitting marbles from the other team away to prevent that team from advancing.

SCORING

The first player or team to complete the course and return back through each hole to the starting hole wins.

Cornhole
United States

HISTORY

The backstory of Cornhole is as tough to pin down as the final airmail toss of a corn kernel-packed bag with the game tied at 20-20. Some say the game's origins date back to 14th century Germany, while others say it originated with the Blackhawk tribe of Illinois in the 1800s that played with pig bladders stuffed with corn. A third theory claims the game originated in the rural Midwest.

The official name of the backyard mainstay has landed at cornhole, but depending on where it's played, the game is referred to lovingly as bean bag, bean toss, soft horseshoes, bags, and Indiana horseshoes.

Cornhole: Throwing Bags in a Hole, the definitive book on the favorite sport of backyard warriors, struggled to pinpoint the exact birthplace or date of the game but praised an unknown and omniscient Genius Farmer for its birth.

The game of Cornhole derived its name simply from the tools of the trade. The traditional version of the game involves palm-sized cloth bags filled with corn kernels to give them weight and wooden boards with holes centered near their backs.

Today, the American Cornhole League states that bags for official play must be filled with plastic resin, but it is not uncommon to find corn-filled bags at Big Ten tailgates and backyard barbecues of the country's Corn Belt.

The game exploded in popularity in the 2000s and has since received airtime on ESPN for the American Cornhole League's World Championships of Cornhole.

The beauty of Cornhole lies in the shallow learning curve for play. It can be easily picked up in an afternoon.

SETUP

Two slanted boards measuring 2 feet by 4 feet should be placed 27 feet apart from the front edge of each other. Each board should be perched up 12 inches at the back and lifted 3 inches at the ground at the front. The boards feature a 6-inch diameter hole drilled nine inches from the back of the board.

The eight bags should measure 6 inches wide by 6 inches long and weigh roughly 1 pound.

31

HOW TO PLAY

2 or 4 players

- Each player, or team, should start with four bags of one color. All bags will begin at one end of the playing field.
- Players from each team will rotate, each throwing one bag at a time toward the opposite board.
- Players must throw from behind the front of the box they are tossing from.
- Players alternate throws until all 8 bags have been thrown.
- If a bag hits the ground, that bag is disqualified. Bags may not roll from the ground onto the board.
- Once all eight bags have been thrown, the players at the other end of the match will begin their round.

SCORING

After all bags have been thrown, any bag remaining on the board is worth 1 point, and bags that went in the hole are worth 3 points. Points are canceled out each round. For example, if one team scored 7 points and the other scored 3, the first team gained a total of 4 points that round.

The game continues until a team reaches 21 points with a lead of 2 or more points.

ESSENTIAL CORNHOLE TERMS

Ace: A bag that lands on the board, 1 point

Airmail: A bag that flies directly into the hole without touching the board

Blocker: A bag that lands on the board and blocks the hole from sliders

Cornhole: A bag that goes into the hole

Corn On The Cob: The result of a player landing every bag on the board

Slider: A bag that slides into the hole

Croquet
England

HISTORY

Like afternoon tea, Mary Poppins, and fish and chips, Croquet is about as British as Her Majesty the Queen. The most proper of backyard sporting games, Croquet even features a suggested dress code consisting of knitted white sweaters. Hats are recommended too.

Like many of the world's yard games, the history of Croquet is murky and has been told through hearsay and rumors over centuries. Some historians trace a primitive version of the game to 12th century France, where peasants played a game in the field consisting of hoops made from willow branches and wooden balls. Others claim an early version of the game more similar to the modern game of Croquet was played in England in the 17th century under the name *paille-maille*, or pall-mall.

Over the years, those willow branch hoops evolved, and in the 1850s, Croquet as we know it exploded in England. Official Croquet sets were manufactured and sold to the middle class during The Great Exhibition of 1851 in London's Hyde Park, and the rest is history.

Croquet was the first Olympic sport to include women when it was featured in the 1900 Summer Olympics in Paris, but unfortunately only lasted one Olympic Games.

Today's game which can be found being played on the pristine green gardens of UK Croquet clubs, but also in the everyman's backyard, is a game of skill and strategy that has taken on multiple game formats: garden Croquet, association, nine-wicket Croquet, six-wicket Croquet, and Golf Croquet. We are going to focus on nine-wicket Croquet, which is often called backyard Croquet, as this is a book focused on the backyard after all.

93. A CURIOUS ANCIENT PASTIME.

SETUP

Players need nine wickets, two stakes, and up to six balls. The official full-size court is a rectangle, 100 feet long by 50 feet wide if you have space. The wickets and stakes should be arranged in a double-diamond pattern. One stake should be placed at each end of the course.

• Players or teams begin at the starting stake, and alternate turns striking their balls through all the wickets on the field. They will navigate through the double-diamond setup in a counterclockwise fashion, but if you don't advance the ball through a wicket, you forfeit your turn.

• Once you hit the turning stake at the opposite end of the court, you follow the opposite side of the diamond back to the starting stake. Once you hit this stake, you win the game!

• If the striker's ball makes it through the wicket, he or she may go again, but the ball must completely clear the wicket to count.

• If the ball rolls through but settles back in place directly under the crossbar, no extra turn is awarded.

• A second shot is also granted to a player if they hit the opposing team's ball on a stroke. In the case both balls stay in contact with each other after the hit, the player may step on their own ball to hold in place and with the mallet transfer a force into the other ball to blast it in any direction.

• The player is granted another turn for this maneuver, and the opponent is left in dismay...

SCORING

The object of the game is to hit your balls through the course of six wickets on the right side to eventually hit the end peg. Next reverse direction and finish by hitting them through the six wickets on the left side and finally strike the starting peg. The team that completes the course first wins.

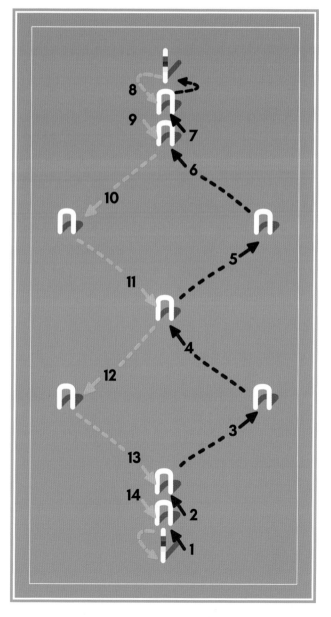

Gaga Ball
Israel

HISTORY

The Thunderdome of Jewish summer camps has pit campers against each other in a close-quarter, dodgeball-like game for decades. Believed to have originated in Israel, Gaga - which translates to "touch touch" in Hebrew - has since made its move across the pond to the United States.

Like dodgeball, Gaga Ball moves quickly, and the purpose of the game is to eliminate players by hitting them with a ball.

The difference in Gaga Ball is that players must strike each other below the knee, and they cannot hold onto the ball. They must slap or whack the ball toward opponents.

Another major difference is the size of the court. Gaga pits are octagonal, tight, and constructed of waist-high walls.

Gaga is not a team sport. It's everyone for themselves in a battle royale inside the mini octagon. The origin of Gaga Ball is believed to be Israel, but the game has exploded in the United States over the past 20 years, primarily in summer camps.

Mediterranean Sea   Israel

SETUP

The biggest need for a proper game of Gaga Ball is the octagonal pit. The sizes of the pit vary, but the walls should be waist-high to keep the ball contained. Gaga Ball can be played with a foam ball, kickball, volleyball, or soccer ball.

HOW TO PLAY

2 - 20 players

• The game begins with players standing along the boundaries of the pit chanting "Ga... Ga... Ball!" followed by one player throwing the ball up in the air and hitting it. Once the ball is in play, players may move around the pit freely.

• Players can hit the ball with an open or closed hand, trying to strike another player's leg below the knee. If a player is hit below the knee, they are out.

• Players can not hold the ball or kick the ball.

• There are no double touches. If a player hits the ball, they can not hit it again until another player touches it or the ball hits the wall.

• If a player hits the ball out of the pit, they are out.

SCORING

Last player standing wins.

39

Hammerschlagen
Germany

HISTORY

A hammer in one hand and an enormous stein filled with the cool beverage of your choice in the other.

This recipe for ... old-fashioned fun originated in Germany sometime between the 1920s and 1940s and has since migrated around the world.

The hardest part about Hammerschlagen, or as it is sometimes known, Nagelbalken, is finding a stump big enough to handle the repetition of nails being smashed into it round after round.

The basis of the game is straightforward. It is a test of one's hammering ability.

Who doesn't like swinging a heavy hammer down on an unsuspecting nail?

As lore has it, the story of Hammerschlagen dates back to a dare made in Germany among friends and a young boy named Carl.

That dare involved a nail game where players originally used an ax to pound a nail into various objects: tires, walls, dirt, and the sides of trees. Each player took their turn taking a swing at the nail until one player finished it into the object. That player was exempt from the next round until there was only one remaining. The loser did the chores.

Young Carl eventually immigrated to Saint Paul, Minnesota, with his family and brought along his new game. This time he swapped the ax for a hammer and the target objects for a stump. The rest is *geschichte*. History.

SETUP

Players need a large stump to play but can substitute a wooden beam, as is custom in Nagelbalken. One hammer is needed and one nail for each player for each round of play.

HOW TO PLAY

2 - unlimited players

• Players surround the stump, and each begins with their own nail in their hand.
The first player starts the game by taking one swing at their nail.

• The game moves around the stump with each player taking one swing at their nail per turn.

• Players must grip the hammer with one hand under the line on the hammer.

• Each swing must be done in a continuous motion. The arc of the swing can be no higher than the player's ear.

• If the nail bends during a turn, the player may use a turn to straighten the nail or attempt to nail it down as-is.

SCORING

The first player to hammer their nail in flush with the stump wins.

Horseshoes
England

HISTORY

A favorite backyard game of dads everywhere, Horseshoes is the godfather of many of the target-based games that have taken the world by storm over the last generation. Like most of the great games of the world, horseshoes is simple in its genius.

It involves no more than throwing its namesake horseshoes at a metal stake in the ground.

The physical object that makes the game great, the horseshoe, dates back to ancient times. A mosaic that was uncovered in Pompeii has a clear depiction of a Horseshoe on a horse. The shoes were and still are meant to protect the hooves of horses during laborious work.

A precursor of today's game is thought to have originated in the second century B.C. in the form of discus throwing in Greece. Well, not everyone could afford these costly discs of discus, so the common man turned to what was available—discarded horseshoes.

Over time the game evolved, and today's version of Horseshoes is thought to have been formalized by the British. The official rules of the game were crafted in England in 1869 and later brought to the United States, where the game was a hit among Civil War soldiers.

SETUP

A Horseshoes pitch features two sides, each with a metal (iron) stake, 40 feet apart.

Stakes should extend 14 to 15 inches above the surface of the pitch. Stakes may be inclined slightly toward each other at an angle of no more than 12 degrees.

Pits at each end should be 31 to 36 inches wide and 43 to 72 inches deep and be filled with clay, sand, soil, or sawdust.

Each pit should have a backboard four feet behind the stake.

HOW TO PLAY

2 or 4 players

• Each player, or team, should start with two horseshoes and toss both shoes consecutively before the player from the opposing team begins.

• The goal is to throw a "ringer" where the horseshoe encircles the stake at the opposite end.

SCORING

Ringers are worth 3 points and are measured by placing a straight edge along the two points of the horseshoe that is encircling the stake. If the edge touches the stake, it is not a ringer.

The closest horseshoe to the stake counts for 1 point. If a player has two shoes closest to the horseshoe, that player is awarded 2 points. If a player from each team scores a ringer, those points are canceled out.

Games are typically played to 21 or 40 points or measured by a time limit on the game.

Irish Road Bowling
Ireland

HISTORY

Irish Road Bowling is a game of epic proportions, and depending on the location of the match, twists, and turns.

Irish Road Bowling, which is also known as bowls, may be one of the most beloved and traditional "yard games" that has lasted to modern times.

Matches can be played on long stretches of roads and last more than an hour.

While official bowling courses created specifically for the game exist throughout Ireland, it is more common to play on makeshift roadway courses.

The first step in playing a proper match of road bowling is finding a suitable course of country roads.

The second is launching a metal ball as fast and hard down that road as you can.

The game may turn into a miniature version of an Easter egg hunt as players search for cannonballs that fly off the roadway.

Road bowling games, which often draw a crowd of spectators and, in turn, bettors, dates back to the 17th century in rural Ireland and are thought to have come to the country via Dutch soldiers.

The game became widespread throughout Ireland in the 19th century but has retreated for the most part to the counties of Cork and Armagh.

The first player to toss their cannonball, called a bowl or bullet, past the finish line on the road in the fewest turns wins.

SETUP

The setup requires nothing more than a road or series of roads and a cannonball for each player or team. The bowl (cannonball) should be 7 inches in diameter and made of iron or steel, and weigh about 1.75 pounds.

Course distances depend on the contest but are typically between 1 to 3 miles.

HOW TO PLAY

2 or 4 players

- Each player or team will start with a bowl behind the starting line.
- Bowlers can run up to the throwing line and must launch the ball in an underhand motion.
- Players should mark the roadway with chalk at the bowls farthest point, not where it went off the roadway.
- A player may loft the bowl over a curve or gap between two roads, but the bowl must strike the roadway. If it does not, the player must take their next turn from the original spot.

SCORING

The player or team to throw their bowl over the finish line in the least number of throws wins. If two players or teams finish in the same number of throws, whichever team's bowl goes further past the finish line wins.

Jogo Da Malha
Portugal

HISTORY

Not to beat a dead horse, but similar to many of the games in our backyard bible, Jogo da Malha traces its roots back to Roman times and—you guessed it—horseshoes.

What differentiates this Portuguese game is that over time players stopped throwing actual horseshoes and exchanged the tossing item for metal discs.

While the thought of throwing discs at a stake in the ground resembles quoits, the goal in Jogo de Malha is to be the first player to knock over the wooden pin.

The Portuguese version is the most common and involves throwing the disc in the air to knock down the stake. There is also a Brazilian version of the game that has gained popularity in which instead of throwing discs in the air, players slide the discs along a slick court on the ground, similar to shuffleboard. Today Jogo da Malha is extremely popular in both Brazil and Portugal.

Additional versions of the game involve setting up multiple stakes known as *belhos* at the end of the playing field.

SETUP

Players set up wooden pins called belhos, which are approximately 6 inches tall and sharpened at one end, in the ground approximately 40 feet apart.

Each team should be equipped with metal discs weighing approximately 1.5 pounds.

HOW TO PLAY

2 or 4 players

- The game may be played one-on-one or in teams of two.
- Players alternate throwing discs toward the wooden pin at the opposite end.

SCORING

The game should be played to 30 points.

3 points are awarded to a player or team that knocks over the belho.

If neither team knocks over the pin, the closest disc to the pin is awarded 1 point.

If the pin is not knocked down and a player has the two closest discs to the pin, that player is awarded 2 points.

Jokgu
Korean Football

Korea

Japan

HISTORY

Jokgu is not for the faint of heart. Or the unathletic. Or those lacking extreme dexterity in their lower limbs.

Imagine a mad scientist fusing together the best of volleyball and soccer. You have Jokgu.

There are two leading theories on the creation of this limb-bending game.

The first is that the game originated in Korea in the 1300s and is the only ball sport born out of the country. This camp argues the similar Southeast Asian game of Takraw was inspired by Jokgu.

An alternative theory states that the game originated in military circles of the Korean Air Force in the 1960s.

Since all men in Korea are required to serve two years in the military, the game quickly spread throughout the country from those military settings.

Under the military theory, the game was said to be devised as a tool to keep the soldiers fit and entertained. The game has since jumped from the world of the armed forces into rec leagues and schools.

Regardless of the true foundation, Jokgu is one of the most popular sports in Korea.

SETUP

Players should set up a net with a height of 3 feet, 7 inches, similar to the height of a tennis court, and mark the playing field 18' by 21'.

The game should be played with an inflated ball slightly harder and smaller than a soccer ball.

HOW TO PLAY

8 players

- Players should form two teams of four players.
- Each point is started with a serve, which must be kicked over the net and into the playing field.
- Players are allowed 3 contacts per side with 1 bounce in between contacts to return the ball over the net. Players may use their feet, shins, or head to contact the ball.
- There are three main offensive techniques used in Jokgu: the standing kick, flying kick, and running kick.

SCORING

Sets are 15 points long. Typical games involve three sets. Teams must win by 2.
Scoring is tallied by the rally system.

KanJam
United States

HISTORY

Relative to other games in this book, KanJam is one of the newer games to catch fire among backyard gamers.

It wasn't until 1999 that the frisbee-based game received its adult name of KanJam, a major step up from the earlier "Garbage Can Frisbee."

The story of Kan and Jam begins in Buffalo, New York, in the 1980s, where college friends created a backyard game that involved throwing a flying disc toward the open mouth of a trash can. The goal was for the throwing player's partner to slap the flying disc into the opening of the can for points.

The founders of KanJam, the official company that began making its own version of the game, trademarked the current setup in 2006.

As the game evolved from its garbage can days, so did the rules. KanJam sets now include a slot on the front of the plastic cylindrical target that acts like a bullseye and is an automatic win if you make it in.

Today, KanJam can be played in pools with special floatable sets, in the dark with a glow-in-the-dark set, and it even comes in a mini tabletop version. The game can now be found in thousands of gym classes in schools across the United States. Countless tournaments are held around the United States each year, including the KanJam World Championship.

SETUP

The official KanJam set includes two portable goals, which are crafted from plastic with a slot in the front.

The goals should be set up 50 feet apart but can be moved closer to improve the quality of play depending on strong winds.

One flying disc is needed for gameplay.

HOW TO PLAY

4 players

• Each team must start with one player on each side of the field of play behind the goal.

• A player from one team will start by throwing the flying disc toward the other end's goal with the hope of hitting the side of the goal with the disc, landing the disc in the top of the goal or in the slot in front of the goal.

• The throwing player's teammate will act as a "deflector" and can tip or slam the flying disc into the goal using one or both hands. Players may not carry or grasp the disc when attempting to redirect it into the goal.

• Players must throw from behind the goal of where they are throwing from.

53

SCORING

1 point is awarded for a "dinger" when the teammate of the throwing player redirects the throw, and the disc hits the side of the goal.

2 points are awarded if the throwing player's toss hits the side of the goal without the help of their teammate.

3 points are awarded when a disc is deflected and lands inside the goal, usually through the top opening.

A team receives an Instant Win if the throwing player's disc goes directly into the slot in the front of the goal.

The first team to 21 wins.

Korbo

Ethiopia

Ethiopia

Africa

HISTORY

In the Horn of Africa, children and adults of Ethiopia have been playing the game of Korbo for more than 100 years.

Although little has been written about the history of the game, it doesn't take long to realize that, like most long-lasting games, Korbo is a game that grew from the utilization of available tools and equipment.

Korbo involves throwing a spear-like stick through a rolling hoop and is thought to have originated as a form of target practice for hunting.

Different versions of the game exist in other neighboring countries, including Kenya and Rwanda, but Korbo has had the most staying power in its home of Ethiopia.

The most common version of the game is played in a field on foot, but the game can also be played on horseback.

Korbo is most popular in the southern regions of Ethiopia and is even played in competitive settings in stadiums.

SETUP

Players need an open space for play and should set up a 45- by 30-foot field of play.

A hoop, typically made of metal or wood, and a spear-like stick with a blunt end are needed for play.

HOW TO PLAY

4 - Unlimited players

• Korbo is played in pairs consisting of one hoop-sender and one spear thrower per team. The sender first rolls the hoop across the playing space while the thrower hurls the spear-like stick toward the rolling hoop from 30 feet away.

• Each team member gets three spear tosses per round. After both players have gone, the other team takes their turn at the game.

SCORING

2 points are awarded if the throw stops the hoop. 1 point is awarded if the throw touches the hoop but does not stop the rolling target. The winning team is that which scores the most points during a match.

Kubb
Sweden

HISTORY

Imagine you have just landed upon the Scandinavian shore alongside your fellow Vikings and, in the name of conquest, soundly defeated a rival village.

The skulls and bones of your enemies lay strewn across the former battlefield. Here began the first game of Kubb (pronounced *koob*) as Vikings began tossing the femur bones of their enemies toward discarded skulls in the wake of victory, according to legend.

Today, "Viking Chess" has cleaned up its act significantly, but the general theme of throwing wooden batons at your opponent's Kubbs (small blocks of wood) still remains.

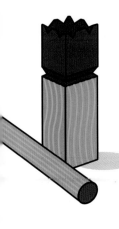

Kubb's origin story, regardless if skulls were involved, runs back through Sweden to the island of Gotland. On that island, the game is called "Kägelkrig" which translates to skittles war.

The goal of Kubb is centered around the king, a wooden piece with a crown, which is placed directly in the middle of the field of play during each match. The end goal is to topple the king.

Players should be cautious in their quest, as if they knock over the king before all of the other Kubbs, they will have already lost the game.

"The brave man well shall fight and win, though dull his blade may be." -from the ancient Viking book of poems, Fafnismal 28.

SETUP

Kubb requires a rectangular field of play, preferably grass, of 8 by 5 meters (~26 ft. x 16 ft).

Five square Kubbs (wooden blocks) should be evenly spaced along each team's end line.

Place the king piece directly in the center of the field of play. A total of six wooden batons are needed for play.

HOW TO PLAY

2 to 12 players

• Players should divide into 2 teams. It is not necessary to have even numbers of players on each team.

• A player from each team shall toss a baton from behind the end line and the team whose baton is closest to the king starts the game.

• Throws must be underhand and spin end-over-end.

- The first team (team A) will begin by throwing their six batons at the opposing team's Kubbs at the other end of the field, trying to knock them down.
- If the king is knocked down, the opposing team automatically wins.
- To start their turn, Team B must first throw any Kubbs which were knocked down by Team A into Team A's half of the field of play. Team A must stand those Kubbs up where they landed.
- If those Kubbs land outside the field of play or don't pass the centerline, they can be re-thrown by Team B.
- Those which had previously been knocked down and later thrown are now "Field Kubbs."
- If neither Team A nor Team B can land the field Kubb in the area of play, Team A can then place them wherever they choose at a minimum of one baton-length away from the king.
- Team B must now knock down all field Kubbs before they can begin attacking the Kubbs along Team A's baseline.
- If any field Kubbs are still standing after Team B has thrown its batons, Team A can throw the batons from a line level with the field Kubb closest to the centerline on their next turn.
- The teams alternate in this fashion until all baseline Kubbs have been knocked down and eventually the king.

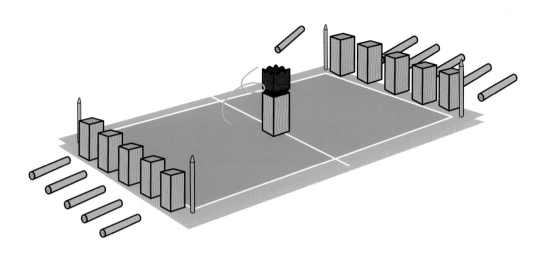

Ladder Toss
United States

HISTORY

Ladder Toss, Norwegian Horseshoes, Bolo Toss, Snakes, Ladder Ball, Bolo Polo, Ladder Golf, Ball Rope … believe it or not, the list actually goes on.

Ladder Toss may have the most nicknames of nearly any of the yard games out there, but the DIY nature of the game has led to a worldwide boom in popularity.

Legend has it that the earliest version of today's bola might have been a live snake thrown at barbed wire fences by cowboys. Points were awarded when the sinister creature wrapped itself around the wire upon contact.

Another more palatable history of the founding of Ladder Toss comes directly from the use of bolas by Gauchos in South America and the cowboys of the Old West. Bolas were a prevalent hunting weapon used to entangle the legs of cattle and other animals. Because of the prevalence of this weapon, it's possible that the game's origins stretch back a few centuries.

It's entirely possible that they used the same weapon for entertainment or simply for practice and that the pastime later evolved into today's game.

Snakes are not easy to throw. Neither are bolas, Ladder Golf´s throwing instrument consisting of two golf balls tied together by rope.

Ladder Toss began to challenge cornhole at college football tailgates in the 2010s and has been a recent entrant into the backyard games canon.

The object of the game is to wrap the bolas around the steps, or rungs, of the three-step ladder.

SETUP

Players need two ladder sets, either from the official retailer Ladder Golf or homemade (a common material for a homemade version is PVC pipe). The ladders should be placed 15 feet apart.

Each player or team must start with three bolas each. The bolas are golf balls or tennis balls with holes drilled in them, connected by a 12-inch piece of thin rope.

HOW TO PLAY

2 or 4 players

• Each player, or team, must start with three bolas of one color at one end.
• Players from each team will rotate, each throwing one bola at a time toward the opposite ladder, trying to wrap the bola around a rung.
• Players must throw from behind the ladder of where they are throwing from.
• There is no set way or rule on how to throw a bola, and bolas may be bounced off the ground.
• Players alternate throws until all six bolas have been tossed.
• Once all six bolas have been thrown, the players at the other end of the match will begin their round.

SCORING

The goal is to throw the bola and have it wrap around a rung. The top rung is worth three points, the second is worth two, and the bottom is worth one.

Players can knock down another team's bolas from the ladder.

In the official version of the game, players play to a hard limit of 21. If a player has 19 points and then throws a bola that lands on the top rung, that player remains at 19 and must reach 21 with a 2 point toss or two 1s.

Lawn Darts
United States

HISTORY

Lawn Darts is the black sheep in the world of yard games.

The game is almost mythical in the backs of the minds of mischievous youth, synonymous with firecrackers and homemade bike ramps.

But should this game really have received its place on the list of banned items of the United States? A report that 6,100 people were sent to the hospital with injuries caused by the deadly flying objects says yes.

Lawn Darts, also known as Javelin Darts, Jarts, Lawn Jarts, and Yard Darts, came to market in the United States in the middle of the 20th century in the form of weighted spikes that players launched into the air toward a plastic circle on the other end of the playing field.

The game resembles some of our favorites including, bags and horseshoes, but includes the added danger of metal spikes falling from the sky.

The game can be dated back to around the third century AD to a weapon of war used by Roman and Greeks called the *plumbatae*.

Lawn Darts was banned by the Consumer Product Safety Commission in 1970, but that ban was overturned when manufacturers agreed not to market the darts as a toy or in toy stores.

That didn't stop players from picking up sets for backyard matches. Tragedy struck in 1987 when an errant dart flew over the fence of a Riverside, California, home and struck a seven-year-old girl in the head, killing her.

The girl's father championed an effort to get the game permanently banned, and he was successful in 1988 following a report that more than 6,000 people had been sent to the hospital for injuries caused by Lawn Darts in the U.S.

Canada followed suit and banned the game in 1989.

Today, it remains impossible to purchase a new set of Lawn Darts for retail stores, but a modified game with blunt plastic tips is available.

SETUP

Keep the Lawn Darts out of reach of children and keep children away from the playing field if playing with metal darts.

Players should place one plastic ring at the starting point, and two target rings roughly 35 to 40 feet away, one inside the other, forming a bulls-eye.

HOW TO PLAY

2 or 4 players

• Players take alternating turns throwing darts during a round.

• A player scores 3 points for landing a dart in the inner ring and 2 points for a dart that lands in the outer ring. One point is awarded for the next closest dart to the outer ring target.

SCORING

Games are played to 21 points.

Mölkky
Finland

Northern Europe   Finland

HISTORY

Finland, the land of clear spirits, warm saunas, and the addicting game of Mölkky! The game, which is quickly becoming a tradition, involves pinpoint accuracy, supreme throwing technique, and the ability to compute third-grade-level arithmetic.

According to its creators, the name Mölkky doesn't truly have any real "meaning," but it does sound very similar to the Finnish word Polkky, which means "a block of wood." Coincidence? I think not. The game is completely made of wood! This isn't just any type of wooden block.

The company that makes Mölkky focuses on environmentally-friendly practices by using scraps of wood from other projects, using completely chemical-free products, and only using natural timber that has been sourced from 100% sustainable Finnish forests. Now that's what I call an eco-friendly game! In 2015, Mölkky even won the Green Toy of the Year Award!

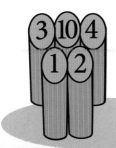

The induction of this game dates back to 1996 when Finnish toy company Lahden Paikka brought it to market. But the true origins date much further back. Möllky is based on the game Kyykka or Finnish Skittles. This game was originally played in the small villages of Karelia, a region between northern Finland and Russia.

Around 1890, during the Kinship Wars, many Karelians migrated to Finland for safety and brought along Kyykkä. For years the sport dwindled, until 1951 when the Finnish president called for a revitalization.

In this game, you throw a bat that is almost 3 feet long at smaller skittles (pins) to knock them out of their own game square. The team that needs the fewest throws wins. Traditionally, the winners of the match get to ride on the backs of the losing team's members.

SETUP

As seen in the picture, all games of Mölkky begin the same way, in a diamond-esc bunch formation. However, after the first throw occurs, no two games are ever the same.

Players throw from 3.5 m (11.5 ft) away. Assuming pins were hit, they are stood back up wherever they are found. That means if one of the pins flies 15 feet away, it will be stood up 15 feet away! This keeps things interesting for every single match.

HOW TO PLAY

2 or 4 players

• Once players have decided who goes first, the throwing commences. The first player will throw the skittle at the grouping of pins and try to knock down as many as possible.

• After the last player has gone, players rearrange the throwing order, with the person with the least amount of points going first and the highest scorer going last.

• If a player should miss any pin three times, they are out for the game.

SCORING

There are two ways to score in Mölkky. If the player knocks only one pin down on the throw, they are awarded the numerical value that is painted at the top of the pin. If a player knocks over two or more pins, then they are awarded one point for every pin that is knocked over. It should be noted that if a pin falls on top of another pin, it does not count as a point.

The pin must lay completely flat on the ground to gain points. Games are played to 50 points, and if you go over that mark, you go all the way back down to 25. In the event of a tie, a Mölkkout occurs.

When this happens, the pins 6, 4, 12, 10, and 8 are set up in a straight line, a skittles distance apart. Then it is basically a best of two throws overtime. Whoever scores the most points wins!

Polish Horseshoes
United States

HISTORY

Up in the Great North of Canada, the Canucks who have taken a liking to this beaut' of a backyard game have dubbed it Beersbee, as it can often be played as a game involving a crispy beverage.

Down south in the United States, the game is more commonly known as Polish Horseshoes or Spanish Horseshoes. In the Midwest, we have Frisbeener, and in Virginia, French Darts.

The point of the game is to throw a flying disc at a bottle that is resting on the top of a pole.

However you call it, the game of Polish Horseshoes is one of the most laid back but challenging of our backyard bible. This game requires snap-fast instincts and killer precision.

To master the art of Polish Horseshoes one must first master the smooth and accurate toss of a flying disc. Secondly, those instincts must be kept sharp as it is imperative that the defender of the post be able to catch a tumbling bottle before it hits the ground.

On top of all of this, the game must be played with only one hand. The other must be holding a bottle or cup at all times.

SETUP

Two poles roughly 5 to 6 feet tall should be stuck into the ground or planted with a base. PVC pipe, tiki torches, or ski poles work well.

The top of the pole should be covered with a small piece of wood or cardboard, tape or other material to create a flat surface to balance a bottle. A bottle should be placed atop each pole, which are spread 20 to 40 feet apart.

HOW TO PLAY

4 players

- Each team will start with both players on the same side of the field of play behind the pole.
- A player from one team will start by throwing the flying disc toward the other end's pole with the goal of either hitting the bottle directly or hitting the pole to cause the bottle to fall.
- Players must stand behind the pole at all times while throwing and catching.
- The defending team must catch the flying disc as well as the bottle if the bottle falls.
- Teammates alternate throwing the disc.

SCORING

1 point is awarded if the defending team drops the flying disc. If the throw is deemed uncatchable, no points are awarded for a drop.
2 points are awarded if the bottle falls and the defending team fails to catch it.
3 points are awarded if the defending team drops both the flying disc and bottle.
The first team to 21 wins. Teams must win by 2.

Quoits
England

NEWCASTLE PIT MEN PLAYING AT QUOITS.

HISTORY

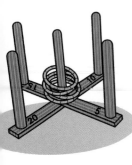

Greek discus seems to have inspired many of the world's traditional lawn games, and England's beloved Quoits is no exception.

Like the majority of the world's great games, Quoits involves throwing an object toward a target. In Quoits, that target is a stake called a hob.

The throwing object of choice in Quoits, a ring. The ring can be made of metal, rope, or rubber. Ring toss may be known as a kids game, but Quoits players want none of that. This is a game of immense skill and passion.

Quoits is thought to be an early predecessor or perhaps cousin to the Yanks' horseshoes and is played in much the same fashion.

The official rules of Quoits were laid down by an official Quoits governing body formed by pubs in 1881 and published in "The Field," the world's oldest country and field sports magazine based in the United Kingdom.

Those rules make up what is today called The Northern Game. Other popular versions of the game include traditional Quoits, the Long Game, and East Anglian Quoits.

For our purposes, we are laying out the setup and rules for The Northern Game, but players may adapt these rules to fit their surroundings and preferences.

SETUP

Two wooden boxes measuring three feet square should be placed 11 yards apart and filled with clay. In the center of each box, place a hob, or iron post, three inches above the surface of the clay.

Eight quoits are needed for play. The quoits are traditionally metal rings measuring 5 ½ inches across and weighing approximately 5 pounds.

HOW TO PLAY

2 to 16 players

• Players form two teams of up to eight players.

• Players from each team take turns throwing the quoits attempting to land the ring over the hob.

SCORING

Games are played to 21 points.

2 points are awarded for a ringer that lands over the hob. Only the top quoit that has ringed the hob is awarded points if multiple players land ringers.

If no player scores a ringer, 1 point is awarded to the team nearest the hob.

If a quoit covers part of the hob but is not a full ringer, that quoit is considered closer to the hob than one that is touching the side of the post.

Ringing the Bull
United Kingdom

HISTORY

Ringing the Bull is a game of the utmost simplicity but at the same time causes extreme frustration for new challengers stepping into the arena of the ring swing.

The most traditional version of Ringing the Bull requires access to a bull horn, a piece of rope or string, and a ring tied to the end. During its hundreds of years of existence, players have bypassed the actual bull horn for hooks on a wall. But, there are many pubs throughout the U.K. and in the Caribbean that feature the authentic version. Often a horn or hook is affixed to the nose or head of another animal such as a deer or pig mounted to a bar's wall.

The history of Ringing the Bull features a storied tale of crusaders and castle guards with too much time on their hands.

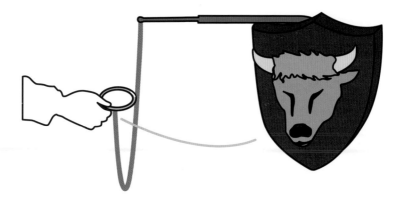

Legend has it that crusaders returning to the United Kingdom from Jerusalem brought the game back to a tavern near Nottingham Castle. That pub aptly named, The Trip to Jerusalem dates back to 1189 and is still open today.

The game, which has a centuries-old history in British pub culture, has more recently immigrated to the United States and other countries around the world.

Since that move, the game has evolved out of the pub setting and into backyard patios and basements everywhere.

For a game that is as simple as swinging a ring at a hook, Ringing the Bull has stood the test of time due to its innately hidden difficulty.

SETUP

Players of Ringing the Bull should attach the target bull horn or hook to a wall at eye height. The hook should be turned upwards.

A 1 to 2 inch in diameter ring should be attached to the end of an 8-foot-long rope, which should be fixed to the ceiling to allow the ring to be swung and be the proper length to catch the hook.

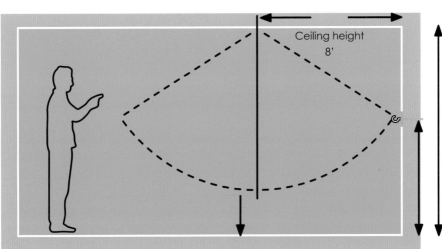

Distance from the wall
5''9''

Ceiling height
8'

18'' from the floor

HOW TO PLAY

2 to 10 players

• The game is typically played by two players, but teams may be formed.

• Each player or team is allowed a specified number of practice swings before beginning the match.

• Players then take turns swinging the ring toward the hook or horn, with each player taking five consecutive swings counting the number of successes.

• Players must swing the ring with an underhand motion but cannot simply drop the ring. A drop can be called out by the competing player and discounted.

• An alternative version of the game can be played in a similar fashion to basketball's HORSE, where players pick spots to throw from or incorporate a special rule such as throwing with the opposite hand or with eyes closed.

SCORING

The first player to 21 hooked rings wins in a traditional game.

Sapo
Peru

HISTORY

The *Sapos* (toads) of the sacred lake of the Incas, Lake Titicaca, were thought to have magical powers. Peruvian legend has it that the royal Inca King, who was the son of the Sun God, brought gold with him when he frequented the lake in an attempt to lure and catch shoreside sapos. According to myth, if a sapo caught a piece of gold in its mouth, whoever threw it would be granted a wish, and the toad would turn to gold.

To honor the magical toad, the king built a golden statue of a great sapo in the gardens of his palace. The king's friends soon created a game of skill revolving around that statue.

The goal of that original game was to land a coin in the statue's mouth.

Today, game boards of Sapo can be found in bars all over Peru. On the center of each board sits a golden toad.

Mirroring the ancient legend of the sapo, the hundreds-of-years-old game involves throwing golden coins toward the toad's mouth.

Since the early days in Peru, the game has traveled by way of Spanish conquistadors back to Europe, where it is still played today.

The game is also popular in South America, specifically in Colombia, Bolivia, and Argentina.

South America

Peru

SETUP

Sapo requires a specialty arcade-like box and board consisting of a brass frog, two spinners, and 20 coins or washer-esque pieces. The surface of the box is arranged into a 4 by 5 pattern of holes (2 in. diameter), and the spinners are usually located over the outer and middle holes in the front row. The spinners resemble the paddle wheel on the back of a steamboat. The surface of the Sapo game can differ between sets and may sometimes have different deflectors on top. Each box is approximately 48 in. by 24 in. by 24 in.

HOW TO PLAY

2 or 4 players

• Each team is given 10 coins to start, and the objective of the game is to land the coins inside the mouth of the frog. Players also score points if the coins land in other holes on top of the box. Each hole is assigned a unique score.

• Players must stand roughly 15 feet from the box, and each player should throw all 10 of their coins consecutively.

• Only coins that enter the top of the box are counted.

• If you land a coin in the toad's mouth, shout, "Sapo!"

SCORING

Each slot on the box has its own point total, including the toad.

The first team to reach an agreed-upon total wins.

Seven Stones
India

HISTORY

The game of Seven Stones, traditionally known as *Pittu Garam* in India, is one of the oldest games continuously played on planet Earth.

The simple rules of Seven Stones and its relatively basic setup and equipment have allowed it to last for five millennia.

Seven Stones, which is also known as *Lagori*, is often played as a team game with as many as a dozen players per side but can be played with as few as two per team.

The overall goal of the game is to break a central "tower" of Seven Stones and reconstruct it as fast as you can before a player from the other team hits you with the ball, usually a tennis ball. In short, Seven Stones is an aggressive game of elusiveness and speed that combines a bit of dodgeball with craftiness.

The game of Seven Stones has a rich history that dates back to the Bhagavad Gita, a 700-verse Sanskrit scripture from the 2nd century B.C. That text describes Lord Krishna, the Hindu deity, playing this ancient game.

Seven Stones is still played in urban and rural parts of India and, despite following a decline in popularity in the early 2000s, has had a resurgence in both India and more than 30 countries around the world thanks to the formation of professional and amateur leagues.

SETUP

Players should set up a pile of seven flat stones, one on top of the other in the center of the field of play, forming a tower. One tennis ball or similarly sized rubber ball is needed for play.

Players should set boundaries in an open area.

Teams should have an even amount of players and should begin equidistant from the stones on either side of the field of play.

HOW TO PLAY

4 - Unlimited players

• A coin toss decides which team will begin the game.

• A player from the team that won the coin toss begins the game by throwing the tennis ball at the pile of stones, attempting to knock over the entire stack of stones.

• The first team gets three attempts to knock over the stones throwing from a set line. If they fail, the second team gets three chances to knock over the pile.

• Once the pile has been toppled, the team that succeeded in their throw must rebuild the pile of stones while trying not to get hit by the ball from the other team.

• The defending team can stop the rebuild by hitting players from the other team with the ball below their knees. Players throwing the ball must throw from where they pick it up and cannot run with it.

• Players on the defending team may pass the ball to their own teammates.

• If a player is hit, they are out of the game. If the attacking team manages to rebuild the pile and trace three circles around it with their finger, they get one point and a chance to throw the ball at the stones again.

• If the defending team gets all players out, they gain a point and are now the attacking team.

SCORING

1 point is awarded to the attacking team if they rebuild the stones and circle the pile with their finger three times.

1 point is awarded to the defending team if they knock out all players on the attacking team before they rebuild the stones.

Players can decide on how many points wins the match.

Spikeball
United States

HISTORY

Spikeball is the love child of volleyball and foursquare.

Of all the backyard games that have popped up in the modern age, it's safe to say Spikeball has gone the most viral at a rapidly increasing rate. The game, which has a cult-like following across college campuses and beyond, has even found its way onto ESPN.

Spikeball has grown to such an extent that many consider that it has evolved from a backyard or seaside hobby into a full-blown sport.

One reason for the craze that is Spikeball is the level of skill, mastery, and creativity that is possible. Spikeball requires players to be quick, agile, coordinated, have speedy reflexes, and communicate seamlessly.

Of course, the game can be picked up by new players in a matter of minutes, but the real action happens when drop shots, diving saves, and slams come into play.

Spikeball is the revival of a failed backyard game from the 1980s that lacked a patent. Chicago-based entrepreneur Chris Ruder revived the game in the 2000s selling sets out of his home and is credited with sparking the worldwide Spikeball movement.

Today the biggest question among Spikeballers is what is the preferred playing surface: sand, grass, or court? Each surface has its own elements that it adds to the game.

HOW TO PLAY

4 players

- Two teams of two should start on either side of the net. All players except for the player receiving the serve must begin at least 6 feet from the net.
- The server must serve the ball down onto the net so that it bounces up toward the receiving player. Once the ball has been served, players may move in any direction they choose. There are no boundaries.
- Possession changes when the ball contacts the net and bounces into the air. The gameplay is similar to volleyball, and each team has up to three touches per possession. A player may not hit the ball twice in a row.

SETUP

Players will need a Spikeball trampoline-like net and an inflated rubber ball with a 12-inch circumference.

The net should be placed in an area with enough room to move freely.

The tension of the net should be consistent throughout.

To test the tension, a ball dropped from 3 feet above the net should bounce up approximately 12 to 18 inches.

SCORING

Spikeball uses rally scoring, meaning points can be won by both the serving and receiving teams. Games are typically played to 11, 15, or 21 and must be won by two points.

Points are awarded when the ball contacts the ground or isn't returned onto the net within 3 touches. If the ball contacts the rim or hits the net and does not bounce off, the opposing team will be awarded a point. 87

Tejo
Colombia

HISTORY

Steel disc and gunpowder don't typically mix well for a fun time with friends, but Colombians have harnessed their power to create what very well may be the most dangerous backyard game in our book.

Tejo, the national sport of Colombia, combines the art of throwing these heavy metal discs with the excitement of blowing up a bag of gunpowder.

The main goal of Tejo is not to directly strike the triangular bags of gunpowder called *mechas* that surround the metal ring known as a *bocin* at the opposite end of the pitch. Still, the crack of the countless micro-explosions during a game is unmistakably thrilling.

The history of Tejo is linked to the indigenous groups in the Colombian municipality of Turmequé, Boyaca, where an early version of the game was born more than 500 years ago, according to official sources.

The game, which is also known as turmequé, was originally played without the element of gunpowder. That element is thought to have been introduced in the 1950s.

Today's game is growing in popularity internationally and was highlighted by Anthony Bourdain during an episode focused on Colombia.

South America

Colombia

SETUP

Two clay or mud-filled boxes are placed at opposite ends of the court approximately 60 feet apart, with a protective backstop behind each box.

An approximately 10 in. diameter pipe is placed in the center of the box at the same 30 to 45 degree angle as the box's pitch.

Each team is equipped with 6 metal discs weighing approximately 2 pounds.

The clay in each box is dotted with packets of gunpowder surrounding the bocin, or metal ring in the middle.

HOW TO PLAY

2 to 12 players

• Players form two teams of up to six players.
• Players take turns throwing the tejos toward the box.
• If a player from one team strikes and explodes a mecha, that round is over, and the winning team of that round gets to start the next.

SCORING

Games are played to 21 or 27 points.

9 points are awarded to a player that explodes a mecha and lands the Tejo in the metal ring or pipe on the same throw.

6 points are awarded to a player who lands a tejo in the ring.

3 points are awarded for exploding a mecha.

1 point is awarded for the tejo closest to the ring at the end of a round.

Washers
United States

HISTORY

While Washers has been called a "poor man's horseshoes," don't count out this rustic game of accuracy.

There are many ways one can throw the washer, which is one of the most exciting parts about this lawn game.

There is the flipper.

There is the Frisbee toss.

There is also the flick.

Washers, which also goes by Washer Toss, Washer Pitching, Ringers, Huachas, and Washoes, has hints of other favorites such as Cornhole and Horseshoes.

All that is technically needed are two cups or holes spread 20 feet apart and a handful of washers from the toolbox.

The official setup and rules have grown more strict as the game has grown in popularity, but the basic setup is all one really needs.

The goal of this game is to throw a washer toward a hole and hope to make it in. It doesn't get any simpler than that.

SETUP

Place two cylindrical objects roughly 20 feet apart. PVC pipe is typically used.

A 16``x 16`` x 4``box around a 4 1/2 x 5`` cylindrical pipe is optional but suggested for more formal play.

Players need two sets of four washers of the same size and weight.

Some versions of the game involve boards with three holes to aim for.

HOW TO PLAY

2 or 4 players

- Each player, or team, starts with four washers
- The first player will toss all four of their washers toward the target.
- The opposing player will then throw all four of their washers.
- The goal is to land the washers inside of the cup or target.

SCORING

Washers that land inside the hole are worth 3 points, and washers that land inside the box are worth 1 point.

Points from each round are tallied and cancel each other out. For example, if player one scores 8 points during a turn and their opponent scored 5, player one will be credited with 3 points.

Games are played to 21 points.

Appendix

Selection Process: It should be noted that the games chosen in this book follow very specific criteria. To be classified as a yard game, it was decided that the game had to have a scoring system, can easily be set up, can be played leisurely without breaking too much of a sweat, and could be played in a park, backyard, beach, parking lot or field type setting with minimal changes to the natural habitat.

Several games were highly debated but may have missed the cut due to the following factors:

1. Too similar to a previously added game. For example, Bocce and Petanque are both very fun and culturally interesting games, but they both have pretty much the same principle of throwing a larger ball as close as possible to a small ball.

2. Games that involved too much energy or were more of a sport than a leisure game. Although yard games and sports have a very close parallel, the aim of this book was to include games that could be played casually. For instance, Jai Alai was more of a sport because of the required equipment needed to play. Ideally, the game can be played while holding a drink of your choice in the other hand.

3. The game is not well enough established.

There are 100s of creative, fun, new, and original yard games on the market that I would have loved to include. Games like these are what keep the competitive spirit high and backyards full in the summertime.

About the Author

Born and raised in the suburbs of Chicago, Matthew Grear is the eldest of two. A late bloomer in life, Matt received his Master's in Healthcare Administration from Cornell University at the ripe age of 29 and now works in healthcare administration at a hospital in Boston. Although there are no parallels for his love of yard games and his career, the stress from his job makes him want to get home even quicker so that he can play yard games for the rest of the evening. Now that's a symbiotic relationship!

The World's Greatest Backyard Games is Matt's first published book to date. However, he does have many other great accomplishments, including 2nd place in high school state football finals, completing a marathon right around a walking pace, and finishing in 2nd place in a bar sanctioned Cornhole tournament. Eventually, he will get 1st place in something, but until that day, you can find Matt hanging outside playing games or traveling the world.

Photo credits